DATING IN MARRIAGE

12 Months of Date Night Ideas,
Discussions Starters, and Check-in Questions

Brittany Noel Putman

For Brian,
My love and best friend in this adventure we call life.

Copyright 2017: BRITTANY PUTMAN

All Rights Reserved.
ISBN-13:978-1544729800
ISBN-10:1544729804

Introduction

I'll never forget my first date with my husband, Brian. Absolutely nothing went according to plan, and it was so much fun! He picked me up and took me to a nearby Cheesecake Factory. First, we couldn't find a parking spot, then we drove around the parking lot for at least 30 minutes before parking in the corner furthest away from the Cheesecake Factory. After a 20-minute hike in heels, we found out that we would have a 3-hour wait to get into the restaurant and so decided to forget about it. By the time we found a place to eat, we were tired, starving, and still happy as clams!

If this happened to Brian and me today, after 2 years of marriage, it would be a completely different story! We would both be angry, and ready to just forget it and go home. So why would we respond differently now compared to when we were dating?

As a new couple, my goal was to impress Brian and show him that I liked him and wanted to be with him despite the circumstances. Now, Brian knows everything about me so I don't have to impress him. I know he loves me no matter what!

So does that mean that we should just settle for ordinary married lives and forget the fun of dating altogether?

No, way! Dating is just as important now as it was when we first met. Dating is fun and it takes you out of the 'everyday' and gives you a place to re-connect and focus on your marriage.

I believe dating is an important part of marriage and that's why I felt the need to share this book with you. Over the next year, this book will take you on a journey to spend one day each month together. Each month you will be presented with a date night idea, a simple devotional, or marriage trait to focus on, and reflection questions. Together, you will make memories that will last a lifetime and make your marriage a priority.

Each monthly date night is unique and requires little planning, so all you need to do is schedule a date and embrace your time together.

I'm so proud of you for investing in your marriage this year. This is going to be so much fun!

Winter Wonderland
January
Intentionality

What better way to kick off the new year than with a fun date night that will leave you cozying up with your spouse. This month, you will be spending time with your spouse while you enjoy a 'Winter Wonderland' date. At first glance, this date is very simple as all you need to do is go play in the snow. But enduring the cold together will take determination and intentionality, just like marriage.

Here are a few things you can do to make the most of your Winter Wonderland Date:

- Walkin' in a Winter Wonderland- Bundle up and take a stroll around town and enjoy the beautiful snow. Throw snowballs or use a stick to write messages in the snow if you like.
- Playing in a Winter Wonderland- Grab a sled and head for the hills. If you don't have a sled, then use cardboard or a plastic lid. Or, go out in your own backyard and build a snowman and an igloo.
- Fighting in a Winter Wonderland- Stage a massive snowball fight. You each get one side of your yard and about 5 minutes to prepare. Play until you have a clear winner.
- No Snow Option- I understand that not everyone lives in an area where you get snow, so here is a 'no snow' option: Pick up 5 or 6 bags of cotton balls before your date night. Use tape or a pretty scarf to make a line right in the middle of your bedroom. Each of you will get half of the 'snowballs.' Have an indoor snowball fight!
- Warming Up Together- After playing in the snow go back inside, clean up, and make some hot chocolate. You can make some basic hot chocolate by mixing 2 tbsp. cocoa, 2 tbsp. sugar, 1 cup milk, and ¼ tsp vanilla in a saucepan and simmer on medium heat until all ingredients have dissolved. Stir in peppermint, caramel, whipped cream or anything else you can dream up, and enjoy. Mix ingredients together in a saucepan and simmer on medium heat until all ingredients have dissolved. Stir in a topping of your choice while the mixture is still hot, and enjoy!

Talk About It: A good marriage doesn't happen overnight; it takes two people who are dedicated to living life together as one. That's why we are talking about intentionality this month. It's the beginning of the year, and I want you to decide right now that you will be intentional in your marriage. Use this book as a guide while you intentionally date your spouse each month. Intentionally pray for each other and your marriage every day. In everything that you do put your marriage and your spouse second only to God.

Reflect Together:

1. Describe this month's date night in one sentence:

2. If you could have a grown-up snow day, how would you spend it?
   Wife's Answer:

   Husband's Answer:

3. What aspect of your life and marriage do you want to remember from this month?

4. How can you intentionally put your marriage first today and every day?

5. Write a prayer, asking God to help you put the things that you wrote about in question 4 into practice. Pray this prayer as many times as necessary over the next month.

Beloved Treasures
February
Treasured

February can only mean one thing: Valentine's Day! Love it or hate it, we are entering the most romantic time of the year. You're probably already thinking about how you will celebrate this holiday. Maybe you even have a Valentine's Day tradition like buying flowers or eating at a special restaurant. This month's date night will center around Valentine's Day and it will be your fanciest date night of the year. Your spouse is a treasure so this month you will treat them like royalty.

Here are a few things that you can do to make the most of your Beloved Treasures Date:

- Wear Your Treasures- Ladies, this is your chance to pull that fancy dress out of your closet and show it off. Wear your nice jewelry. Fellas, this is your chance to dress up as well. Why not try a nice tie or at least a dress-shirt? It's only for one night!
- Eat Like Royalty- You don't have to go to the most expensive restaurant in town, but go somewhere nice. Why not try somewhere new?
- Act Like Treasures- Go out and play the part. Treat yourselves like royalty. Husbands, open car doors for your wife and splurge for steak and dessert if you feel like it. This is the only 'fancy' date night in this book so it's okay to indulge just a little.
- See A Show- You're already dressed up so why not see a show while you're out? This could be a play, or the orchestra, or really anything you want it to be.

Talk About It: Your spouse is one of the greatest gifts that God will ever give you. This is a person who knows you better than anyone else in the world. They know that you always leave socks on the floor and how annoying you become whenever you are sick, and they love you anyway. Your spouse is truly a treasure. So this month you will be focusing on treasuring each other. It's easy to take the person you love for granted, but this month all that is going to change. What changes do you need to make in order to treat your spouse like a treasure?

Reflect Together:

1. Describe this month's date night in one sentence:

2. If you could have any physical treasure in the world, what would it be?
   Wife's Answer:

   Husband's Answer:

3. What aspect of your life and marriage do you want to remember from this month?

4. How can you treasure your marriage and your spouse today?

5. Write a prayer, asking God to help you put the things that you wrote about in question 4 into practice. Pray this prayer as many times as necessary over the next month.

Looking Up
March
Putting God First

As the old saying goes: March is in like a lion and out like a lamb. You just never know if March will be snow showers or warm, sunny afternoons. This month, you will embark on a date night that will have you 'Looking Up' as you reach for the skies. In marriage, you should always be looking up and praying up. Whenever you put God first you'll be amazed at what happens in your life. This month, you will focus on putting God first in your marriage.

Here are a few things that you can do to make the most of your Looking Up Date Night:

- Kite Contest- Head to your local dollar store and pick up a few kites. It's completely fine to get the *Finding Nemo* and *Barbie* kites if you want them! Head to a local park, and find a nice open area for kite flying. Challenge each other to see who can keep the kite in the air the longest and who can high their kite the highest. Whoever loses has to cook dinner that night!
- Fly a Drone- Drones are all the rage right now, so if you have one take if out and learn to fly it. See if you can get some cool pictures together from the drone.
- Looking Up- Spend some time discussing God's role in your marriage and make a commitment to put God first in all areas of your life. The questions below will help you with this.
- Fly Higher- Take this date night to the next level by scheduling a hot air balloon or helicopter ride. This is completely optional but really, what's more romantic than a hot air balloon ride?

Talk About It: The institution of marriage was created as a picture of how Christ loves the church. The church anticipates the coming of Christ, just like a bride anticipates marrying her new husband. Whenever God is first in your marriage, it will be different than any other self-seeking relationship that you may have. Whenever you put God first in your relationship you will focus on what God wants for your life instead of what you want, which in turn means that you are united as one. The Bible teaches that a 'cord of three is not easily broken' so protect your marriage today by putting God first.

Reflect Together:

1. Describe this month's date night in one sentence:

2. What does your relationship with God look like, both in marriage and personally?
   Wife's Answer:

   Husband's Answer:

3. What aspect of your life and marriage do you want to remember from this month?

4. How can you put God first in your marriage today?

5. Write a prayer, asking God to help you put the things that you wrote about in question 4 into practice. Pray this prayer as many times as necessary over the next month.

Glamping
April
Respect

Camping is fun, but Glamping gives you the opportunity to enjoy a little camping fun without even leaving your living room. In order to be a successful camper, you need to know what you are doing. You do not want to find yourself in the middle of the woods without a compass or a way to cook your dinner! There are certain skills you need to know in order go camping without harming yourself - like knowing how to start a fire! The same is true in marriage. This month, you are going to focus on respect. Respect is the ability to disagree with your spouse without belittling their opinions and ideas.

Here are a few things that you can do to make the most of your Glamping Date Night:

- Pitch a Tent- Pull out all your blankets make yourself a tent in your living room. Stretch a fitted sheet over the top of two chairs to make a roof. Cover the floor with pillows and more blankets. Turn the lights down low and snuggle up together.
- Share Campfire Stories- While you snuggle up in your tent, share campfire stories. Make up your own stories or google a few to read out loud. Or throw in a movie. Just make sure you enjoy it all from your cozy glamping tent.
- Indoor S'mores- Make S'mores by spreading graham crackers on a baking sheet and then placing chocolate on the graham cracker. Top with a marshmallow. Bake in the oven until the marshmallows start to brown and the chocolate starts melting.
- Sleeping Under the Stars- If you are brave, spend the night sleeping under the stars inside your tent. You won't have real starlight, but you can hang Christmas lights if you want.

Talk About It: Do you love or hate glamping? Do you both agree or disagree on this issue? In marriage, disagreements are going to happen. In fact, they may happen often and over silly things that don't seem worthy of argument. Disagreements should be expected, but it's how you treat your spouse during the disagreement that really matters. You must value your spouse enough to respect them even whenever they are completely wrong. It means controlling your behavior, listening to their opinions, and being ok with the fact they don't agree with you. Respect is hard because it requires us to let a little bit of our ego go. Respect and love go hand in hand. If you truly love someone then it will show through in how you treat them.

Reflect Together:

1. Describe this month's date night in one sentence:

2. Tell your favorite camping memories. Why do you love or hate camping?
   Wife's Answer:

   Husband's Answer:

3. What aspect of your life and marriage do you want to remember from this month?

4. How can you show respect to your spouse? Are there any issues relating to respect that you need to discuss now?

5. Write a prayer, asking God to help you put the things that you wrote about in question 4 into practice. Pray this prayer as many times as necessary over the next month.

Staying On Course
May
Refresh

May is finally here, the flowers are blooming and there's no better time to spend as much time outside as possible. In fact, flowers would be a lovely way to begin your May date night! (I'm looking at you, husbands!) This month, you are heading to the nearest miniature golf course where you'll enjoy some time together while you soak up the beginning of summer and spring's most beautiful flowers. This date night requires no prep-other than driving to the golf course and is the perfect way to refresh your marriage and have a little fun.

Here are a few things that you can do to make the most of your Staying On Course Date Night:

- Traditional Mini Golf- Head to your local miniature golf course and see who has the best mini golf skills. Make it a contest. The loser has to wash the dishes for a week or fold that mountain of laundry that has been sitting on the couch for a little too long.
- Glow Golf- Instead of enjoying an outdoor date night, find a glow-in-the-dark golf course. Many malls have these.
- Marathon Mini Golf- Instead of just playing one game of miniature golf, have a marathon. Visit as many mini golf courses as you can in one day and play a round at each course. Rank them and determine which mini golf course is the best one in town.
- No Golf Course? No Problem- If you live in a small town like me, and there isn't a miniature golf course available, then you can make your own mini golf course in your back yard. Cut several large plastic cups in half and tape them to the floor. Make lanes and courses out of tape as well. Use a broom as your putter and any small ball that you can find. And there you have it: your own miniature golf course.

Talk About It: May is a breath of fresh air after a cold and snowy winter. Sometimes, our marriages need a 'refresher' as well. When you're dating or newly married, everything is fresh and exciting. However, after a few years, you may feel yourselves falling into a rut. You can refresh your marriage by spending time together and remembering why you fell in love with each other in the first place. Date nights are a great way to hit 'refresh' on your marriage, so if you are reading this book, then you've taken the first step towards keeping the magic alive in your marriage!

Reflect Together:

1. Describe this month's date night in one sentence:

2. Why did you fall in love with your spouse? What first attracted you to him/her?
   Wife's Answer:

   Husband's Answer:

3. What aspect of your life and marriage do you want to remember from this month?

4. Does your marriage need to be refreshed? What can you do this month to freshen up your marriage?

5. Write a prayer, asking God to help you put the things that you wrote about in question 4 into practice. Pray this prayer as many times as necessary over the next month.

Hoops and Cones
June
Balance

The very first Valentine's Day gift that I gave my husband was a basketball. He loved playing basketball before we were married so I thought maybe we could play together every now and then. It was a great gift and I've had lots of fun playing basketball with him, even though I always lose! This month, you will have your own basketball adventure! This may or may not be your favorite game to play, but this month is all about balancing your hobbies and time with your spouse so you'll be playing basketball and then going out for ice cream!

Here are a few things that you can do to make the most of your Hoops and Cones Date Night:

- Find a Court- Head to a local park where you can shoot hoops. Spend some time shooting hoops, or play one-on-one.
- Horse- If your skills aren't quite up to playing an actual game, then play horse. Horse is a fun game that will take you back to your childhood.
- Pick Your Own Sport- If basketball isn't really your jam, then pick your own sport to play together.
- Ice Cream- After your basketball date, head to your local ice cream parlor and enjoy some ice cream together. While you enjoy your treat, talk about how you spend your time. Does your marriage have a healthy balance of 'me time' and 'we time?'

Talk About It: Sometimes, husbands and wives have the same interests and hobbies and sometimes they don't. One thing that everyone new couple struggles with is finding a balance between spending time together and doing their own thing. This is different for every couple but the principles are the same: Put your spouse first, but have something that is just yours. It's okay to spend an evening pursuing your hobbies once in a while, as long as you realize that your family is more important than your hobbies.

Reflect Together:

1. Describe this month's date night in one sentence:

2. If you could spend one day doing anything without interruption, what would you do?
   Wife's Answer:

   Husband's Answer:

3. What aspect of your life and marriage do you want to remember from this month?

4. Are you spending a healthy amount of time together and doing your own thing? What do you need to change, if anything, to make your time more balanced?

5. Write a prayer, asking God to help you put the things that you wrote about in question 4 into practice. Pray this prayer as many times as necessary over the next month.

Just Keep Swimming
July
Endurance

Whenever I think of July, I think of the sun, sunscreen, and waves, so your July date night will be all about jumping in the water and cooling off! If you are lucky enough to live near the ocean. then pack a bag and head out for the day. If not, find a local swimming pool, or pick up a few water guns! This date night can be as simple or complicated as you make it. It's up to you! The main point is that you get out and spend a romantic day together in the sun.

Here are a few things that you can do to make the most of your Just Keep Swimming Date Night:

- Find a Beach- Go to the beach and spend the day swimming, sunning, boating, surfing, and enjoying your time with your spouse.
- Find a Pool- If you don't live near the beach, find a pool. Maybe you have one in your backyard, or maybe there is one in town. Spend the day hanging out at the pool, splashing around and soaking up the sun! Don't forget the sunscreen!
- Water Gun Fight- Pick up a few water guns or water balloons and have a little competition.
- Fish Instead- Not a fan of swimming? Go fishing instead! Fishing is a great way to relax and have some good conversation while you wait for the fish to bite.
- Under the Sea Movie- Once you are exhausted from a full day of swimming, curl up on the couch and watch a water-related movie. A few good ones would be *Finding Nemo, Castaway,* or *Jaws!*

Talk About It: If you've even been caught in a strong current while swimming then you know that swimming takes endurance. You see the shoreline in the distance and all you can do is keep swimming until your feet hit the sand. Whenever you marry someone, you marry them 'for better or for worse.' I wish I could tell you that it's always better but that's just not the case. Hard times will come if they haven't already. Whenever they do you'll need the endurance to keep focusing on your spouse. Even when they are wrong and being downright unlovable! When hard times come, remember why you love your spouse and don't give up on them. Remember to pray together often to help endure the hard times. You will come out stronger than ever before.

Reflect Together:

1. Describe this month's date night in one sentence:

2. Share your best summer memories from when you were a child.
   Wife's Answer:

   Husband's Answer:

3. What aspect of your life and marriage do you want to remember from this month?

4. What hard times have you endured as a couple? What got you through it? What would you do different next time?

5. Write a prayer, asking God to help you put the things that you wrote about in question 4 into practice. Pray this prayer as many times as necessary over the next month.

Reach for the Stars
August
Forever

Have you ever sat outside at night and just stared at the stars? Whenever you consider how vast our universe is, you realize that your world is very small. But no matter how big or little your world may seem, the person sitting at the center of your universe is your spouse. Your spouse is the one who knows all your flaws and loves you anyway. I believe that marriage is forever and that you can work through any issue as long as you cherish your spouse above all else and follow God's leading. This month, you will Reach for the Stars as you celebrate spending forever with your spouse.

Here are a few things that you can do to make the most of your Reach for the Stars Date Night:

- Cozy Stargazing- Sit outside on a clear night and watch the stars. See how many constellations you can identify, and spend the evening telling your spouse how much you love them. Fill a kiddie pool with pillows and blankets and light citronella candles to keep the bugs away and create a romantic atmosphere.
- Name a Star- Visit www.StarRegistry.com and name your very own star. There is a fee, but it's still a very cool thing to do.
- Identify the Stars- Download an app like Star Map, to find and identify the stars and constellations around you.
- Visit a Planetarium - Visit a Planetarium and let a professional show you the stars.
- Have a *Star Wars* Date Night- Relax on the couch and watch your favorite Star Wars movie, or make it a marathon and watch all the movies.

Talk About It: One of the cool things about stars is that they last for a very long time. In fact, because they are so far away and it takes a very long time for their light to get to us, the stars that we see today are really only shadows of what they used to be. Likewise, I want you to love your spouse so deeply that the legacy that you leave behind shines through your children, your grandchildren, and forever. You can make your love last forever by how you treat each other. Show them how much they mean to you through how you treat them. Consider each other's feelings and respect each other's opinions even whenever you disagree. Find ways to bring closure to a conflict without degrading their character. Put your spouse on a pedestal and treasure them above all else. Never forget why you fell in love and always follow God's direction for your lives.

Reflect Together:

1. Describe this month's date night in one sentence:

2. Would you ever consider traveling to space? Do you think living in space is something that will be possible in your lifetime?
   Wife's Answer:

   Husband's Answer:

3. What aspect of your life and marriage do you want to remember from this month?

4. What would your family/friends say about your relationship? Do you treat each other in a way that makes others believe that your relationship will last forever? What, if anything, do you need to change now so that your marriage will last forever?

5. Write a prayer, asking God to help you put the things that you wrote about in question 4 into practice. Pray this prayer as many times as necessary over the next month.

Treasure Hunt
September
Forgiveness

Who doesn't love a treasure hunt? For this month's date night, you will dig through what some would call trash in search of a treasure. That's right, you are headed to a local thrift store. There a few different ways to make this date night a success so make sure to check out the options below. This month, you will focus on forgiveness and its role in your marriage.

Here are a few things that you can do to make the most of your Treasure Hunt Date Night:

- Trashy Date Picnic- Head to your local Goodwill. You will purchase everything that you need for this date night at Goodwill! Start by picking out outfits for each other. Bonus points if you find shoes and accessories for each other as well. Then, find a blanket that will serve as your picnic blanket. Finally, find some new dishes and a basket for your picnic and you're ready to go! Wash all of your clothes and dishes and then head to the park for your own trashy picnic.
- Treasure Hunt- If you or your spouse as a specific item that they collect, such as McCoy pottery or old comic books, spend the day searching for some real treasure. Research the best flea markets to visit and see how many real treasures that you can find!
- Trashy Gifts- Head over to your favorite second-hand shop and see who can find the best gift for the other person without leaving the store. You will have 20 dollars and 20 minutes to make it happen.
- Beachy Treasures- If you live near the beach, grab a metal detector and head down to the beach early in the morning to see what treasures you can find there.
- Watch *National Treasure*- Finish your date night off with a fun, treasure hunting movie!

Talk About It: No matter where this date night took you, you found a way to take something that was old, and give it new life. One way that you can give your marriage new life is through forgiveness. 1 Corinthians 13 teaches us that love forgives and it's really as simple and plain as that. Whenever possible, but your pride aside and forgive your spouse so that you can move on.

Reflect Together:

1. Describe this month's date night in one sentence:

2. What would your perfect gift be?
   Wife's Answer:

   Husband's Answer:

3. What aspect of your life and marriage do you want to remember from this month?

4. Are you holding on to anything that needs to be forgiven? Do you need to ask your spouse for forgiveness about anything? Do you consider yourself to be a good forgiver?

5. Write a prayer, asking God to help you put the things that you wrote about in question 4 into practice. Pray this prayer as many times as necessary over the next month.

Beautiful Changes
October
Change

Whenever I think of October, I think of beauty. In the spring, trees bud and new life is born. In the summer, trees live and grow. But it is in the fall that they give the world a glorious show when their leaves change colors and cover the ground in a blanket of orange, red, and yellow. In marriage, you will go through different seasons of life as well. Some seasons will be full of life and new beginnings, like moving to a new city, or having a baby. Other seasons will seem mundane and others will be a struggle. Expect change, because will come. This month you will enjoy a date night that will send you to view nature's beauty while you think about how your marriage has changed this year.

Here are a few things that you can do to make the most of your Beautiful Changes Date Night:

- Take a Drive- Fill your car up with gas and drive down a scenic road. Stop whenever you find an interesting shop or park. Find a place to eat somewhere along the way. Listen to good music and enjoy a peaceful drive together.
- Strike a Pose- The changing leaves make a beautiful background for family photos, so hire a photographer and have professional pictures taken.
- Have the Full Fall Experience- Go to a Pumpkin Farm and have the full Fall Festival experience. Wander through a corn maze, pick pumpkins, take a hayride, and try some yummy pumpkin treats.
- Take a Hike- Throw on your hiking boots and spend the day in the woods chatting and taking in the beautiful colors.

Talk About It: Our lives are ever changing and that's a good thing! You probably aren't the same person that you were when you were as a child, a teenager, or even on your wedding day. One day you may wake up and realize that the person you fell in love with has changed. Hopefully, they have changed for the better! The only thing that won't change is God's desire for your marriage to be a reflection of His love for His people. As changes happen, you will have to decide how to handle them. You can meet them with adversity and fear, or with confidence in God and your spouse. Take time look back and celebrate all of the changes that you and your spouse have faced!

Reflect Together:

1. Describe this month's date night in one sentence:

2. How have you changed since your wedding day?
   Wife's Answer:

   Husband's Answer:

3. What aspect of your life and marriage do you want to remember from this month?

4. Does change frighten you? Has change put a strain on your marriage or your relationship with God? Are there any changes that you need to discuss with your spouse today?

5. Write a prayer, asking God to help you put the things that you wrote about in question 4 into practice. Pray this prayer as many times as necessary over the next month.

Marathons and Fondue
November
Communication

In November, you are most likely focusing on two things: Thanksgiving and the upcoming holiday season. November's date night will give you a chance to rest and catch up with your spouse before the busyness sets in. This date night will take a whole day, but feel free to shorten it if necessary. First, you will have a movie marathon. Pick a movie series that you absolutely love or really want to see and spend the whole day watching those movies and cuddling up with your family. Pair this date night with fondue for dinner so that you are mixing a familiar movie marathon with a fun new dinner idea. This month we are talking about communication so don't be afraid to share your opinions about the movie and the fondue.

Here are a few things that you can do to make the most of your Marathons and Fondue Date Night:

- Take the Marathon Challenge- Watch your favorite movie and its sequels back to back! Pick something that both spouses like and stock up on lots of coffee, snacks, and blankets before you begin watching your movies. You could pick: *Star Wars, Lord of the Rings, Indiana Jones, Rocky, Spiderman, Jurassic Park, Back to the Future*, or anything else that you and your spouse agree on.
- Marathon TV Show- Netflix makes it easy to have a TV Show Marathon. Pick a favorite TV show and watch an entire season together.
- Try Fondue- After your first movie, melt a bowl of cheese and dip various foods into it, such as bread, chips, pretzels, chicken, smoked sausage, veggies, and fruits. Use this meal time as a break from your movies, or eat it while you watch. After your second movie, melt chocolate and try chocolate fondue. Try your chocolate fondue with many different foods such as popcorn, apples, oranges, strawberries, marshmallows, cookies, or anything else that you want to try dipped in chocolate. If you don't have a fondue pot you can easily melt your cheese and chocolate in the microwave or on the stove.
- Don't forget to share your opinions about your movies and fondue!

Talk About It: Communication is the starting point of your relationship and the first way in which you connect with your spouse. You are constantly communicating, whether you realize it or not, with your body language, words, and even your silence. Strong marriages require strong communication skills. You need to really listen to each other and try to understand what your spouse needs. Miscommunication can lead to fights and hurt feelings, so always assume the best of your spouse and ask for clarification before you respond.

Reflect Together:

1. Describe this month's date night in one sentence:

2. If your life was made into a movie series, what would it be about? What would it be called?
   Wife's Answer:

   Husband's Answer:

3. What aspect of your life and marriage do you want to remember from this month?

4. Are you good communicators? What can you do to improve communication in your marriage? Do you have a strategy to help you hand miscommunications?

5. Write a prayer, asking God to help you put the things that you wrote about in question 4 into practice. Pray this prayer as many times as necessary over the next month.

It's Christmastime
December
Joy

It's Christmas! Which also means it's the busiest time of the year. I strongly encourage you to find time for a date night amongst the shopping, cookie baking, and Christmas parties. This date night is a little different than the others because I'm leaving it up to you to decide exactly what you want to do. This month we are talking about joy because Christmas fills me with joy the same way I hope your spouse fills you with joy!

Here are a few things that you can do to make the most of your Christmas Date Night:

- Christmas Lights- Jump in your car and find the best light displays in town.
- Christmas Shopping and Cocoa- If you must, make Christmas shopping a date night in itself. Shop until you are done, and then grab a cup of coffee or dinner together.
- Christmas Movie at Home- If you're exhausted and all you want to do is stay home, then sit on the couch and watch your favorite Christmas movie.
- Christmas Church Service or Play- Find a local Christmas service or play and make it into your very own date night.
- Christmas Cookie Baking Contest- If you and your spouse are fond of cooking, then have a cookie baking contest. The loser has to do all the dishes while the winner samples the cookies!
- Christmas Party- Go to a nice Christmas party, just the two of you! Dress up and enjoy a night out.

Talk About It: Christmastime is when we celebrate the miracle of Jesus' birth and His promise of salvation. Jesus paves a way for us to have eternal life with God and that is the most joyous gift we will ever receive. While marriage isn't all happiness and roses, I do hope that your spouse brings you joy. I hope that you laugh together and play together, that you continue to date no matter how long you have been married! Your spouse is a gift from God. Show your appreciation to God by treating your spouse with love and kindness.

Reflect Together:

1. Describe this month's date night in one sentence:

2. What does joy look like for you? What brings you joy?
   Wife's Answer:

   Husband's Answer:

3. What aspect of your life and marriage do you want to remember from this month?

4. How do you bring joy to your spouse? How does your spouse bring joy to you? Is there anything in your marriage that needs to change so that you both will be filled with more joy?

5. Write a prayer, asking God to help you put the things that you wrote about in question 4 into practice. Pray this prayer as many times as necessary over the next month.

Marriage Retreat for Two

Congratulations! If you have made it to this page then you have invested in your marriage for an entire year by putting your marriage first. I hope that you have learned a wealth of knowledge about your spouse and I hope that you have had fun.

Now here's the best part: This is only the beginning! In the next year, it's up to you what you do and where you take your marriage. It is my hope that you will continue dating and reflecting on your marriage. But before we move on to a new year and I set you free to do this on your own, I have one more task for you and it's going to be a good one.

You are going to embark on a marriage retreat for two! Where and when you go is completely up to you! However, I suggest that you plan your trip within 3 months of finishing this book so that you don't forget. Go somewhere that makes you both happy, whether it be a bed and breakfast right in your backyard, or a beach a thousand miles away. I suggest making this a 1 or 2-night trip, and that you go by yourselves.

Once you get to your destination, you will have 3 short sessions to read and 3 easy tasks to complete.

Now, go and plan your dream getaway!

Congratulations! I am so proud of you for putting your marriage first and planning a marriage retreat. This is going to be so much fun! Soak up every minute of your retreat and enjoy the company of your spouse.

Session 1
Past

Focal Point: I want you to remember the first time that you ever looked at your spouse and thought that this was the person that you wanted to marry. Did your stomach fill with butterflies? Did you blush and hold your breath as you asked them out? Falling in love is exciting! Today, we are going to try to capture those feeling again.

Challenge: Take turns telling the story of whenever you first fell in love. Try to remember the feelings and excitement of it. Now, go out and pretend that you are on your first date all over again. Go out of your way to open your date's car door (hopefully you do this every day!) and dress to impress. Where you go is completely up to you!

Reflect: Use these questions as conversation starters, you don't have to write anything down unless you want to.

How has life changed since you first fell in love with your spouse?
Is your relationship stronger now than it was then? Why?
What did you love most about them then and what do you love most about them now?

Session 2
Present

Focal Point: What stage of life are you in right now? Are you newlyweds? Raising little children? Empty nesters? Today I want you to focus on where you are right now. Take a look at your spouse and think about everything that they do for you and your family. What do you love about them right now? Today, we are going to think about where your marriage is right now and celebrate it.

Challenge: Go and do something that you've never done before. This might be skydiving, or it might be eating sushi! It's completely up to you!

Reflect: Use these questions as conversation starters, you don't have to write anything down unless you want to.

What do you love about your spouse right now?
What is most challenging about this stage of life? How can you support each other through this challenge?
What can you do today to show your spouse love and support?
What little, day to day arguments are holding you back from happiness right now? How can you resolve this issue?

Session 3
Future

Focal Point: Think about the future. Where do you see yourself and your marriage in 5 years? 10 years? 50 years? What you do today is the foundation of your future. Put first things first by focusing on what really matters and put your time and attention there.

Challenge: Grab a pen and paper and write down your goals for your marriage and family for the next year, for the next 5 years, and the next 10 years. Now is the time to ask what you want out of life and make a plan to get there. Do you want to take a family vacation to Disney World? Then you better start planning now. Do you want your children to be raised in church? Find a good church now. Do you want to build a house of your own? What do you need to do to make this happen? Don't try to plan out every detail of the next few years of your life, but instead, make sure that you are on the same page and working for the same things.

Reflect: Use these questions as conversation starters, you don't have to write anything down unless you want to.

How does setting and working towards common goals strengthen your marriage and prepare you for the future?
Do you have any personal dreams that are yet to be fulfilled? How can your spouse help you fulfill your dream?
What changes do you need to make now, so that you can meet the goals you wrote about today?

Brittany Putman is the creator and writer of GraceLoveLife.com, where she encourages wives to build strong, Godly homes by practicing grace and celebrating love in everyday life. *Dating in Marriage* is her first book. She currently lives in Kentucky with her husband and two dogs. They treasure every minute that they get to spend together and with their extended family.

If you need more creative date night ideas check out:
gracelovelife.com/category/marriage/date-ideas/

Printed in Poland
by Amazon Fulfillment
Poland Sp. z o.o., Wrocław